When BOB Met WOODY

Written by Gary Golio & illustrated by Marc Burckhardt

LITTLE, BROWN AND COMPANY

New York   Boston

"ALL I CAN DO IS BE ME, WHOEVER THAT IS."
—BOB DYLAN

MAY 1941

Bob floated into this world on waves of sound.

In the city of Duluth,
on the shore of Lake Superior,
in the cold North Country of Minnesota.

To the music of ships' bells, seagulls' cries,
and the rhythm of rumbling freight cars, young
Bob Zimmerman began his life story.

Bob's ears were open to everything around him. He'd listen for the booming foghorns in the harbor, calling out from the great gray ships hidden in the mist.

He loved the songs that came from the radio. At four, he performed one at a family party.

"If everyone in this room will keep quiet," he said, "I will sing for my grandmother."

When the crowd yelled for an encore, Mom couldn't stop smiling at her brilliant, blue-eyed boy.

Not long after that, the Zimmermans moved to Hibbing, Minnesota, a mining town near Canada. They were one of the few Jewish families in town.

There, during the long winters, Bob watched the northern lights dance in the night sky.

In summer, he and his friends rode their bikes to the mine, spying on the tiny trucks and men, hundreds of feet below.

When Bob was ten, a cousin tried to teach him piano, but he hated taking lessons.

"I'm going to play the piano the way I want to," he said, and taught himself piano *and* guitar.

In town, the whistle of each passing train called to Bob. He'd sit down by the tracks, count the steaming locomotives, and dream of hitching a ride to some faraway place.

To the clank of railroad cars carrying iron ore, he'd make up poems and songs. At home, he'd write little stories, with himself as the hero.

When Hibbing's miners went on strike, Bob saw real-life heroes: everyday people standing up and speaking out to win their cause.

At twelve years old, Bob listened to far-off radio stations
late into the night.

From Chicago, he heard songs by black musicians whose records
you couldn't even buy in Hibbing. Guitarists like Muddy Waters and
B. B. King lit up the airwaves with fiery feelings and sizzling notes.
Bob's fingers itched to play the blues.

From stations farther south, he soaked up the bittersweet ballads of Hank Williams, the lovesick cowboy. With just a few simple words, Hank's songs made him feel *so lonesome he could cry.*

Bob's parents were hardworking businesspeople. Helping Dad in the store, Bob earned spending money for records and an electric guitar.

But Dad didn't care for Bob's music and thought playing the guitar was a waste of time. Bob felt like they lived in two different worlds.

By the time he was fourteen, Bob was playing
guitar and piano with a few close friends
almost every day.

He even talked about being a musician when he grew up, but no one took him seriously. People in Hibbing either worked in the mine or ran their own businesses. They expected their kids to do the same.

More and more, Bob felt like an outsider in his own hometown. One night, he just stood under a streetlight with his guitar, singing to the falling snow.

Teased for being Jewish, for being *different*, Bob kept his angry feelings locked inside.

But when he first heard Elvis Presley— the King of Rock 'n' Roll—it was "like busting out of jail." With his band The Shadow Blasters, Bob let loose onstage, banging the piano and screaming out words to "Dizzy Miss Lizzie" or "Jailhouse Rock."

Some kids called him *crazy*.

During a school talent show, Bob and his band got kicked off stage for being too loud. Afterward, Bob swore he'd be a *music star* one day—even bigger than Elvis—and show them all!

Bob kept listening to all kinds of music, from hillbilly to jazz. He read poems by Dylan Thomas, and books like John Steinbeck's *The Grapes of Wrath*, about poor Oklahoma farmers during the Great Depression. Like ships' horns in the harbor, the world was calling out to him.

When Bob graduated from high school, an uncle gave him a stack of records by Lead Belly, a black folksinger who sang about the struggle for justice and the search for truth. Bob wanted to use the power of music like that, too—even if his parents hoped he'd be an engineer.

> "FOLK MUSIC WAS ALL I NEEDED TO EXIST."
> —BOB DYLAN

To please Mom and Dad, Bob started college in nearby Minneapolis. He went to classes but spent most of his time in Dinkytown, where young people met in coffeehouses and folk music was all the rage.

To Bob, folk music seemed pure and honest, with songs about real life, hard times, and hope.

After hearing a record by Odetta—a young folksinger with a voice like a wildcat—he traded in his electric guitar for an acoustic. When a café owner asked his name during an audition, he suddenly answered, "Bob—Bob *Dylan*," after his favorite poet.

He was starting a new life, with a new name.

Onstage at the Purple Onion, Bob tried to sing clearly, to tell the story in each song. He sounded so bad at first that people walked out.

So he practiced day and night, learning sea chanteys, railroad songs, mountain ballads, and fiddle tunes. He'd fall asleep with the guitar in his lap, and he'd even forget to bathe or brush his teeth.

And then, one day, he heard the records of Woody Guthrie.

"WOODY MADE EACH WORD COUNT. HE PAINTED WITH WORDS."
—BOB DYLAN

Woody was everything Bob wanted to be: a roamin' and ramblin' singer and storyteller who'd played for striking miners and starving farmers. He was from Oklahoma, straight out of Steinbeck's *Grapes of Wrath*, and he had written more than a thousand songs—about dust storms and tornadoes, heroes, hobos, and gunslinging outlaws. He played country, blues, *and* folk music. His song "This Land Is Your Land" was a national favorite.

When Bob read Woody's book *Bound for Glory*, it was like finding the North Star in the night sky. Woody's words were a compass, pointing the way to a bigger, brighter world.

Now Bob yearned to write songs like Woody, to make people think and feel. He wanted *so much* to be like Woody that he pretended to be an orphan from Oklahoma, a runaway, a street singer who'd done his share of "hard travelin'."

"ALL I GOT IS MY GUITAR AND THAT LITTLE KNAPSACK. THAT'S ALL I NEED."
—BOB DYLAN

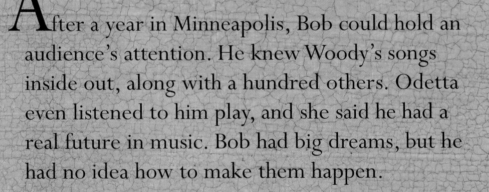

After a year in Minneapolis, Bob could hold an audience's attention. He knew Woody's songs inside out, along with a hundred others. Odetta even listened to him play, and she said he had a real future in music. Bob had big dreams, but he had no idea how to make them happen.

Then he heard that Woody was alive—and very ill—in a hospital outside New York City. Bob got the number and called.

"I'm coming out there," he told the nurse. "Tell Woody I'm coming out to see him."

Bob hitchhiked to New York in January
1961. The city lay frozen under a foot of
snow, and Bob didn't know a soul. He was
nineteen years old.

Carrying his guitar, Bob walked into a
Greenwich Village club and asked to play
some songs. When he got the OK, he
jumped up onstage.

"Name's Bob Dylan," he said. "Been travelin'
around the country. Followin' in Woody
Guthrie's footsteps."

Rough around the edges, Bob had a boyish
charm. The audience really liked him, and
someone even let him sleep on their couch
that night.

A few days later, Bob hopped a bus to Greystone Hospital.

When he got there, what he saw surprised him. Woody was thin and shaky, his traveling days long over. He could talk only in a whisper, but he offered Bob a smile.

So Bob did what came naturally. He sang
Woody's songs while Woody sat and
listened, his eyes sparkling.

Promising to come back, Bob
left that day with a card
from Woody that read,

"Ain't dead yet."

Bob went back to visit his hero, and Woody looked forward to seeing "the boy."

A few weeks later, Woody's family invited Bob to visit him at a friend's house, on a trip out of the hospital. The room was filled with world-famous musicians and folksingers.

Bob sat at Woody's feet. Strumming the guitar, he quietly began singing a song he'd written, and a hush fell over the room. "Song to Woody" was Bob's first real folk song—a gift to his hero and friend.

Hey hey, Woody Guthrie, I wrote you a song…

When Bob finished, Woody's face lit up like the sun.

That night, Bob walked back through the cold streets, filled with a warm glow. After following in Woody's footsteps, he was ready to blaze a trail of his own, to set down his thoughts and feelings in song.

SONGS ABOUT REAL LIFE,
HARD TIMES, AND HOPE.

SONGS THAT MOVED PEOPLE TO
SPEAK OUT AND STAND UP.

SONGS ABOUT THE STRUGGLE
FOR PEACE AND JUSTICE.

SONGS IN A NEW VOICE,
FOR A NEW TIME.

"I WAS JUST DOING WHAT I COULD WITH WHAT I HAD WHERE I WAS."
—BOB DYLAN

AFTERWORD

Bob Dylan has said that when he came to New York City in 1961, he was a "Woody Guthrie jukebox," able to play all of Woody's recorded songs.

By meeting Woody, Bob came to know some of the most talented and important figures in American folk music—people like Pete Seeger, Joan Baez, Ramblin' Jack Elliott, and Dave Van Ronk. Impressed with Bob's ability and enthusiasm, many of these musicians influenced Bob and helped him find work singing in clubs and cafés. Often, they fed him meals and lent him their couches, too.

Bob was quite a storyteller when he met Woody, claiming that he was an orphan, a runaway who'd worked as a carnival roadie, a student of Chicago street singers, and a studio musician who'd played on some Elvis Presley records. But Bob was charming, and friends knew that his stories were harmless and often hilarious. As folksinger Dave Van Ronk once said, "We accepted him not because of the things he said he had done but because we respected him as a performer."

As Bob quickly became part of the Greenwich Village music scene, many friends and fellow musicians became his devoted fans, encouraging club owners to give him greater opportunities. In September 1961, less than eight months after arriving in New York, Bob performed at Gerde's Folk City. He was the lead act, and the *New York Times* gave him a glowing review. A few weeks later, Bob signed a contract with Columbia Records. It was the beginning of a long career.

Bob Dylan has been called "the voice of a generation" and "America's troubadour," names that he thinks are silly. Songs like "Blowin' in the Wind," "Masters of War," and "The Times They Are A-Changin'" were adopted by the civil rights movement, and many have inspired calls for peace worldwide. Bob's ability to meld different musical styles—folk, rock, and blues among them—has changed the face of popular music. His song "Like a Rolling Stone" was chosen by critics and musicians, just a few years ago, as the number one rock 'n' roll song of all time.*

After recording nearly fifty in-studio and live albums, Bob Dylan still performs up to one hundred concerts each year to enthusiastic audiences around the world.

Rolling Stone magazine, December 9, 2004

Sources & Resources

Books

Cohen, John. *Young Bob: John Cohen's Early Photographs of Bob Dylan*. New York: powerHouse Books, 2003.

Dylan, Bob. *Chronicles: Volume One*. New York: Simon & Schuster, 2004.

Dylan, Bob, and Barry Miles. *Bob Dylan in His Own Words*. Edited by Pearce Marchbank. New York: Quick Fox, 1978.

Scaduto, Anthony. *Bob Dylan: An Intimate Biography*. New York: Grosset & Dunlap, 1971.

Sounes, Howard. *Down the Highway: The Life of Bob Dylan*. New York: Grove Press, 2001.

Audio

Dylan, Bob. *Bob Dylan*. [CD] New York: Columbia Records, 1962/2003.

Dylan, Bob. *Greatest Hits, Volumes 1 & 2*. [CD] New York: Columbia Records, 1967/1971.

Folkways Records. *A Vision Shared: A Tribute to Woody Guthrie and Leadbelly*. [CD] New York: Columbia Records, 1988.

Guthrie, Woody. *A Tribute to Woody Guthrie*. [CD] Burbank, CA: Warner Brothers, 1989.

Video

A&E Entertainment. *Bob Dylan: The American Troubadour*. [DVD] Arts and Entertainment Cable Network. New York: A&E Home Video, 2000.

Pennebaker Hegedus Films. *Bob Dylan: Don't Look Back*. [DVD] New York: Crush Digital Video: Distributed by New Video, 1999.

Sony Music. *A Vision Shared: A Tribute to Woody Guthrie and Leadbelly*. [DVD] New York: Sony Music: Manufactured by Columbia Music Video, 1988.

Internet

Interactive website for fans of Bob Dylan, http://www.bobdylan.com.

Author's Note

As a boy, I was always looking for heroes, just as Bob was looking for Woody even before he'd ever heard of him. Babe Ruth, Leonardo da Vinci, Spider-Man, Amelia Earhart, and Harry Houdini—they were just a few of my inner stars, and I came to them for guidance, hoping to learn some of life's secrets. But it was Bob's search for *his* guiding star that inspired me to write this book.

More than anything, I wanted to write a story that told the *truth*. Starting out, I read a lot of books and articles, watched a ton of videos, listened to piles of CDs (and vinyl records!), and pieced together the parts of Bob's life that I thought were interesting. I dug deep into Bob's "roots"—where he came from, what his hometown and family were like, and what *he* felt was important growing up—and tried to let a story grow on its own from there. But only when I read about Bob writing his "Song to Woody"—using one of Woody's own melodies, a practice common in folk music—did I know where my story was going and why Woody was so important to Bob. That's when all the pieces fell into place, even though there was still plenty of "writing work" left to do.

Anyone reading this story should also know that the details of Bob's early life are sometimes remembered differently by different people. For example, did he hitchhike his way to New York, or really catch a ride with a friend? Should you believe Bob's own version of what happened, just because he said it? In the end, certain facts "rang true" to me, and sometimes I let Bob have the last word because it's his life. That's also why you'll find quotes in parts of the book to bring us closer to Bob's own thoughts and feelings.

Finally, if we could all meet our heroes—even in our imagination—maybe we'd understand our own stories better and who we really want to be. To learn more about Bob and Woody, just listen to their songs. It's all there in the music.

Quotation Notes ～～～～～～～～～～～～～

"All I can do is be me": interview with Bob Dylan, *Los Angeles Free Press*, September 17 and 24, 1965.

"If everyone in this room": Sounes, *Down the Highway*, p. 15. (From interviews with Bob's parents by Robert Shelton in *No Direction Home: The Life and Music of Bob Dylan*.)

"I'm going to play": Sounes, *Down the Highway*, p. 20.

"so lonesome he could cry": a reference to Hank Williams's classic song "I'm So Lonesome I Could Cry."

"like busting out of jail": Sounes, *Down the Highway*, p. 27. The full quote is: "When I first heard Elvis's voice I just knew that I wasn't going to work for anybody and nobody was gonna be my boss…. Hearing him for the first time was like busting out of jail."

"Folk music was all I needed": Dylan, *Chronicles: Volume One*, p. 236.

"Bob—Bob *Dylan*": Scaduto, *Bob Dylan: An Intimate Biography*, p. 27.

"Woody made each word count": Dylan, *Chronicles: Volume One*, p. 247.

"hard travelin'": from the lyrics of a song by Woody Guthrie, "Hard Travelin'."

"All I got is my guitar": Scaduto, *Bob Dylan: An Intimate Biography*, p. 52.

"I'm coming out there": Sounes, *Down the Highway*, p. 65.

"Name's Bob Dylan": Sounes, *Down the Highway*, p. 76.

"Ain't dead yet": Sounes, *Down the Highway*, p. 79.

"the boy": Scaduto, *Bob Dylan: An Intimate Biography*, p. 56.

"I was just doing what I could with what I had where I was": Dylan, *Chronicles: Volume One*, pp. 252–53.

"Bobby Dylan…": Scaduto, *Bob Dylan: An Intimate Biography*, p. 56.

"BOBBY DYLAN IS A FOLK SINGER…. HE'S A FOLK SINGER ALL RIGHT."
—WOODY GUTHRIE

To all my teachers, young and old
—G.G.

To my partner in love and life, Janice
—M.B.

Little, Brown and Company • Hachette Book Group • 237 Park Avenue, New York, NY 10017
Visit our website at www.lb-kids.com

Little, Brown and Company is a division of Hachette Book Group, Inc.
The Little, Brown name and logo are trademarks of Hachette Book Group, Inc.

The publisher is not responsible for websites (or their content) that are not owned by the publisher.

First Edition: May 2011

Library of Congress Cataloging-in-Publication Data

Golio, Gary.
When Bob met Woody : the story of the young Bob Dylan / by Gary Golio ; illustrated by Marc Burckhardt. — 1st ed.
p. cm.
Includes bibliographical references and index.
ISBN 978-0-316-11299-4 (alk. paper)
1. Dylan, Bob, 1941— — Juvenile literature. 2. Rock musicians — United States — Biography — Juvenile literature.
3. Guthrie, Woody, 1912–1967 — Juvenile literature. I. Burckhardt, Marc, 1962– ill. II. Title.
ML3930.D97G65 2011   782.42164092 — dc22
[B]   2010043030

10 9 8 7 6 5 4 3 2 1
SC
Printed in China

The illustrations for this book were done in acrylic and oil on paper mounted on board.
The text was set in Perpetua, and the display type was hand-lettered by the illustrator.